Eat That Frog!

21 Great Ways to Stop Procrastinating and Get More Done in Less Time

Brian Tracy

Published by Simple Truths LLC
1952 McDowell Road, Suite 205
Naperville, IL 60563-6506

Design: Design Resource Center, Naperville, IL

Printed and bound in the United States of America.

www.simpletruths.com
(800) 900-3427

ISBN 978-1-60810-019-4

05 WOZ 10

Table of Contents

Introduction: Eat That Frog

This is a wonderful time to be alive. There have never been more possibilities and opportunities for you to achieve more of your goals than exist today. As perhaps never before in human history, you are actually drowning in options. In fact, there are so many good things that you can do, that your ability to decide among them may be the critical determinant of what you accomplish in life.

If you are like most people today, you are overwhelmed with too much to do and too little time. As you struggle to get caught up, new tasks and responsibilities just keep rolling in, like the waves of the ocean. Because of this, you will never be able to do everything you have to do. You will never be caught up. You will always be behind in some of your tasks and responsibilities, and probably in many of them.

The Need to Be Selective

For this reason, and perhaps more than ever before, your ability to select your most important task at each moment, and then to get started on that task and to get it done both quickly and well, will probably have more of an impact on your success than any other quality or skill you can develop.

An average person who develops the habit of setting clear priorities and getting important tasks completed quickly will run circles around a genius who talks a lot and makes wonderful plans but who gets very little done.

The Truth About Frogs

Mark Twain once said that if the first thing you do each morning is to eat a live frog, you can go through the day with the satisfaction of knowing that that is probably the worst thing that is going to happen to you all day long.

Your "frog" is your biggest, most important task, the one you are most likely to procrastinate on if you don't do something about it. It is also the one task that can have the greatest positive impact on your life and results at the moment.

The first rule of frog eating is this:
If you have to eat two frogs, eat the ugliest one first.

This is another way of saying that if you have two important tasks before you, start with the biggest, hardest, and most important task first. Discipline yourself to begin immediately and then to persist until the task is complete before you go on to something else.

Think of this as a test. Treat it like a personal challenge. Resist the temptation to start with the easier task. Continually remind yourself that one of the most important decisions you make each day is what you will do immediately and what you will do later, if you do it at all.

The second rule of frog eating is this:
*If you have to eat a live frog at all, it doesn't pay
to sit and look at it for very long.*

The key to reaching high levels of performance and productivity is to develop the lifelong habit of tackling your major task first thing each morning. You must develop the routine of "eating your frog" before you do anything else and without taking too much time to think about it.

Take Action Immediately

In study after study of men and women who get paid more and promoted faster, the quality of "action orientation" stands out as the most observable and consistent behavior they demonstrate in everything they do. Successful, effective people are those who launch directly into their major tasks and then discipline themselves to work steadily and single-mindedly until those tasks are complete.

Develop the Habits of Success

Your success in life and work will be determined by the kinds of habits that you develop over time. The habit of setting priorities, overcoming procrastination, and getting on with your most important task is a mental and physical skill. As such, this habit is learnable through practice and repetition, over and over again, until it locks into your subconscious mind and becomes a permanent part of your behavior. Once it becomes a habit, it becomes both automatic and easy to do.

Whenever you complete a task of any size or importance, you feel a surge of energy, enthusiasm, and self-esteem. The more important the completed task, the happier, more confident, and more powerful you feel about yourself and your world.

The completion of an important task triggers the release of *endorphins* in your brain. These endorphins give you a natural "high". The endorphin rush that follows successful completion of any task makes you feel more positive, personable, creative, and confident.

The Three D's of New Habit Formation

You need three key qualities to develop the habits of focus and concentration, which are all learnable. They are decision, discipline, and determination.

First, make a *decision* to develop the habit of task completion. Second, *discipline* yourself to practice the principles you are about to learn over and over until they become automatic. And third, back everything you do with *determination* until the habit is locked in and becomes a permanent part of your personality.

Visualize Yourself as You Want to Be

There is a special way that you can accelerate your progress toward becoming the highly productive, effective, efficient person that you want to be. It consists of your thinking continually about the rewards and benefits of being an action-oriented, fast-moving, and focused person. See yourself as the kind of person who gets important jobs done quickly and well on a consistent basis.

Your mental picture of yourself has a powerful effect on your behavior. Visualize yourself as the person you intend to be in the future. Your self-image, the way you see yourself on the inside, largely determines your performance on the outside. All improvements in your *outer* life begin with improvements on the *inside*, in your mental pictures.

You have a virtually unlimited ability to learn and develop new skills, habits, and abilities. When you train yourself, through repetition and practice, to overcome procrastination and get your most important tasks completed quickly, you will move yourself onto the fast track in your life and career and step on the accelerator.

Eat That Frog!

There is one quality that one must possess to win, and that is definiteness of purpose, the knowledge of what one wants and a burning desire to achieve it.

Napoleon Hill

Chapter 1

Set the Table

Before you can determine your "frog" and get on with the job of eating it, you have to decide exactly what you want to achieve in each area of your life. *Clarity* is perhaps the most important concept in personal productivity. The number one reason why some people get more work done faster is because they are absolutely clear about their goals and objectives, and they don't deviate from them. The greater clarity you have regarding what you want and the steps you will have to take to achieve it, the easier it will be for you to overcome procrastination, eat your frog, and complete the task before you.

A major reason for procrastination and lack of motivation is vagueness, confusion, and fuzzy-mindedness about what you are trying to do and in what order and for what reason. You must avoid this common condition with all your strength by striving for even greater clarity in your major goals and tasks.

Here is a great rule for success:
Think on paper.

Only about 3 percent of adults have clear, written goals. These people accomplish five or ten times as much as people of equal or better education and ability but who, for whatever reason, have never taken the time to write out exactly what they want.

There is a powerful formula for setting and achieving goals that you can use for the rest of your life. It consists of seven simple steps. Any one of these steps can double and triple your productivity if you are not currently using it. Many of my graduates have increased their incomes dramatically in a matter of a few years, or even a few months, with this simple, seven-part method.

1 Step one: ***Decide exactly what you want.*** Either decide for yourself or sit down with your boss and discuss your goals and objectives until you are crystal clear about what is expected of you and in what order of priority. It is amazing how many people are working away, day after day, on low-value tasks because they have not had this critical discussion with their managers.

2 Step two: ***Write it down.*** Think on paper. When you write down a goal, you crystallize it and give it tangible form. You create something that you can touch and see. On the other hand, a goal or objective that is not in writing is merely a wish or a fantasy. It has no energy behind it.

3 Step three: ***Set a deadline on your goal; set sub deadlines if necessary.*** A goal or decision without a deadline has no urgency. It has no real beginning or end. Without a definite deadline, you will naturally procrastinate and get very little done.

4 Step four: *Make a list of everything that you can think of that you are going to have to do to achieve your goal.* As you think of new activities, add them to your list. Keep building your list until it is complete. A list gives you a visual picture of the larger task or objective. It gives you a track to run on.

5 Step five: *Organize the list into a plan.* Organize your list by priority and sequence. Take a few minutes to decide what you need to do first and what you can do later. With a written goal and an organized plan of action, you will be far more productive and efficient than people who are carrying their goals around in their minds.

6 Step six: *Take action on your plan immediately.* Do something. Do anything. An average plan vigorously executed is far better than a brilliant plan on which nothing is done. For you to achieve any kind of success, execution is everything.

7 Step seven: ***Resolve to do something every single day that moves you toward your major goal.*** Build this activity into your daily schedule. You may decide to read a specific number of pages on a key subject. You may call on a specific number of prospects or customers. You may engage in a specific period of physical exercise. Whatever it is, you must never miss a day.

Keep pushing forward. Once you start moving, keep moving. Don't stop. This decision, this discipline alone, can dramatically increase your speed of goal accomplishment and boost your personal productivity.

The Power of Written Goals

Clear, written goals have a wonderful effect on your thinking. They motivate you and galvanize you into action. They stimulate your creativity, release your energy, and help you to overcome procrastination as much as any other factor.

Goals are the fuel in the furnace of achievement. The bigger your goals and the clearer they are, the more excited you become about achieving them. The more you think about your goals, the greater becomes your inner drive and desire to accomplish them.

Think about your goals and review them daily. Every morning when you begin, take action on the most important task you can accomplish to achieve your most important goal at the moment.

*Planning is bringing the future into the present
so that you can do something about it now.*

Alan Lakein

Chapter 2

Plan Every Day In Advance

You have heard the old question, "How do you eat an elephant?" The answer is "One bite at a time!"

How do you eat your biggest, ugliest frog? The same way; you break it down into specific step-by-step activities and then you start on the first one.

Your mind, your ability to think, plan, and decide, is your most powerful tool for overcoming procrastination and increasing your productivity. Your ability to set goals, make plans, and take action on them determines the course of your life.

Conversely, as Alec Mackenzie wrote, *"Taking action without thinking things through is a prime source of problems."*

Increase Your Return on Energy

One of your top goals at work should be for you to get the highest possible return on your investment of mental, emotional, and physical energy. The good news is that every minute spent in planning saves as many as ten minutes in execution. It takes only about 10 to 12 minutes for you to plan out your day, but this small investment of time will save you up to two hours (100 to 120 minutes) in wasted time and diffused effort throughout the day.

You may have heard of the Six-P Formula. It says, "Proper Prior Planning Prevents Poor Performance."

Six-P Formula

"*Proper Prior Planning Prevents Poor Performance*"

When you consider how helpful planning can be in increasing your productivity and performance, it is amazing how few people practice it every single day. And planning is really quite simple to do. All you need is a piece of paper and a pen. The most sophisticated Palm Pilot, computer program, or time planner is based on the same principle. It is based on your sitting down and making a list of everything you have to do before you begin.

Two Extra Hours per Day

Always work from a list. When something new comes up, add it to the list before you do it. You can increase your productivity and output by 25 percent or more – about two hours a day – from the first day that you begin working consistently from a list.

Make your list the night before for the workday ahead. Move everything that you have not yet accomplished onto your list for the coming day, and then add everything that you have to do the next day. When you make your list the night before, your subconscious mind will work on your list all night long while you sleep. Often you will wake up with great ideas and insights that you can use to get your job done faster and better than you had initially thought.

The more time you take to make written lists of everything you have to do, in advance, the more effective and efficient you will be.

We always have time enough, if we will but use it aright.
Johann Wolfgang Von Goethe

Chapter 3

Apply the 80/20 Rule to Everything

The 80/20 Rule is one of the most helpful of all concepts of time and life management. It is also called the "Pareto Principle" after its founder, the Italian economist Vilfredo Pareto, who first wrote about it in 1895. Pareto noticed that people in his society seemed to divide naturally into what he called the "vital few", the top 20 percent in terms of money and influence, and the "trivial many", the bottom 80 percent.

He later discovered that virtually all economic activity was subject to this principle as well. For example, this principle says that 20 percent of your activities will account for 80 percent of your results, 20 percent of your customers will account for 80 percent of your sales, 20 percent of your products or services will account for 80 percent of your profits, 20 percent of your tasks will account for 80 percent of the value of what you do, and so on. This means that if you have a list of ten items to do, two of those items will turn out to be worth five or ten times or more than the other eight items put together.

Number of Tasks Versus Importance of Tasks

Here is an interesting discovery. Each of the ten tasks may take the same amount of time to accomplish. But one or two of those tasks will contribute five or ten times the value of any of the others.

Often, one item on a list of ten tasks that you have to do can be worth more than all the other *nine* items put together. This task is invariably the frog that you should eat first.

Focus on Activities, Not Accomplishments

The most valuable tasks you can do each day are often the hardest and most complex. But the payoff and rewards for completing these tasks efficiently can be tremendous. For this reason, you must adamantly refuse to work on tasks in the bottom 80 percent while you still have tasks in the top 20 percent left to be done.

Before you begin work, always ask yourself, "Is this task in the top 20 percent of my activities or in the bottom 80 percent?"

The hardest part of any important task is getting started on it in the first place. Once you actually begin work on a valuable task, you will be naturally motivated to continue. A part of your mind loves to be busy working on significant tasks that can really make a difference. Your job is to feed this part of your mind continually.

Motivate Yourself

Just *thinking* about starting and finishing an important task motivates you and helps you to overcome procrastination. Time management is really *life* management, personal management. It is really taking control of the *sequence of events*. Time management is having control over what you do next. And you are always free to choose the task that you will do next. Your ability to choose between the important and the unimportant is the key determinant of your success in life and work.

Effective, productive people discipline themselves to start on the most important task that is before them. They force themselves to eat that frog, whatever it is. As a result, they accomplish vastly more than the average person and are much happier as a result. This should be your way of working as well.

Every great man has become great, every successful man has succeeded, in proportion as he has confined his powers to one particular channel.

Orison Swett Marden

Chapter 4

Consider the Consequences

The mark of the superior thinker is his or her ability to accurately predict the consequences of doing or not doing something. The potential consequences of any task or activity are the key determinants of how important a task really is to you and to your company. This way of evaluating the significance of a task is how you determine what your next frog really is.

Dr. Edward Banfield of Harvard University, after more than fifty years of research, concluded that "long-term perspective" is the most accurate single predictor of upward social and economic mobility in America. Long-term perspective turns out to be more important than family background, education, race, intelligence, connections, or virtually any other single factor in determining your success in life and at work.

Your attitude toward time, your "time horizon", has an enormous impact on your behavior and your choices. People who take a long view of their lives and careers always seem to make much better decisions about their time and activities than people who give very little thought to the future.

Successful people have a clear *future orientation*. They think five, ten, and twenty years out into the future. They analyze their choices and behaviors in the present to make sure that what they are doing today is consistent with the long-term future that they desire.

Make Better Decisions About Time

In your work, having a clear idea of what is really important to you in the long term makes it much easier for you to make better decisions about your priorities in the short term.

By definition, something that is important has long-term potential consequences. Something that is unimportant has few or no long-term potential consequences. Before starting on anything, you should always ask yourself, *"What are the potential consequences of doing or not doing this task?"*

Rule: *Future intent influences and often determines present actions.*

The clearer you are about your future intentions, the greater influence that clarity will have on what you do in the moment. With a clear long-term vision, you are much more capable of evaluating an activity in the present to ensure that it is consistent with where you truly want to end up.

Obey the Law of Forced Efficiency

The law of Forced Efficiency says that "There is never enough time to do everything, but there is always enough time to do the most important thing." Put another way, you cannot eat every tadpole and frog in the pond, but you can eat the biggest and ugliest one, and that will be enough, at least for the time being.

You cannot eat every tadpole and frog in the pond, but you can eat the biggest and ugliest one.

Three Questions for Maximum Productivity

You can use three questions on a regular basis to keep yourself focused on completing your most important tasks on schedule.

1 The first question is *"What are my highest value activities?"* Put another way, what are the biggest frogs that you have to eat to make the greatest contribution to your organization? To your family? To your life in general?

2 The second question you can ask continually is *"What can I, and only I, do that if done well will make a real difference?"* This question came from the late Peter Drucker, the management guru. It is one of the best of all questions for achieving personal effectiveness. What can you and only you do that if done well can make a real difference?

3 The third question you can ask is, *"What is the most valuable use of my time right now?"* In other words, "What is my biggest frog of all at this moment?"

This is the core question of time management. Answering this question correctly is the key to overcoming procrastination and becoming a highly productive person. Every hour of every day, one task represents the most valuable use of your time at that moment. Your job is to ask yourself this question, over and over again, and to always be working on the answer to it, whatever it is.

The more accurate your answers are to these three questions, the easier it will be for you to set clear priorities, to overcome procrastination, and to get started on that one activity that represents the most valuable use of your time.

Make time for getting big tasks done every day. Plan your daily workload in advance. Single out the relatively few small jobs that absclutely must be done immediately in the morning. Then go directly to the big tasks and pursue them to completion.

Boardroom Reports

Chapter 5

Practice Creative Procrastination

Creative procrastination is one of the most effective of all personal performance techniques. It can change your life.

The fact is that you can't do everything that you have to do. You have to procrastinate on *something*. Therefore, procrastinate on small tasks. Put off eating smaller or less ugly frogs. Eat the biggest and ugliest frogs before anything else. Do the worst first!

Everyone procrastinates. The difference between high performers and low performers is largely determined by what they choose to procrastinate on.

Since you must procrastinate anyway, decide today to procrastinate on low-value activities. Decide to procrastinate on, outsource, delegate, and eliminate those activities that don't make much of a contribution to your life in any case. Get rid of the tadpoles and focus on the frogs.

Learn To Say... No!

One of the most powerful of all words in time management is the word no! Say it politely. Say it clearly so that there are no misunderstandings. Say it regularly as a normal part of your time management vocabulary.

Say no to anything that is not a high-value use of your time and your life. Say no graciously but firmly to avoid agreeing to something against your will. Say it early and say it often. Remember that you have no spare time. As we say, "Your dance card is full."

> "Say no to anything that is not a high-value use of your time and your life."

For you to do something new, you must complete or stop doing something old. Getting in requires getting out. Picking up means putting down.

Creative procrastination is the act of thoughtfully and deliberately deciding upon the exact things you are not going to do right now, if ever.

Procrastinate on Purpose

Most people engage in *unconscious* procrastination. They procrastinate without thinking about it. As a result, they procrastinate on the big, valuable, important tasks that can have significant long-term consequences in their lives and careers. You must avoid this common tendency at all costs.

Your job is to deliberately procrastinate on tasks that are of low value so that you have more time for tasks that can make a big difference in your life and work. Continually review your duties and responsibilities to identify time-consuming tasks and activities that you can abandon with no real loss. This is an ongoing responsibility for you that never ends.

For example, a friend of mine was an avid golfer when he was single. He liked to golf three or four times a week, three to four hours each time. Over a period of years, he started a business, got married, and had two children. But he still played golf three to four times a week until he finally realized that his time on the golf course was causing him enormous stress at home and at the office. Only by abandoning most of his golf games could he get his life back under control.

The first law of success is concentration—to bend all the energies to one point, and to go directly to that point, looking neither to the right nor to the left.

William Mathews

Chapter 6

Use the ABCDE Method Continually

The more thought you invest in planning and setting priorities before you begin, the more important things you will do and the faster you will get them done once you get started. The more important and valuable a task is to you, the more likely you will be motivated to overcome procrastination and launch yourself into the job.

The ABCDE Method is a powerful priority setting technique that you can use every single day. This technique is so simple and effective that it can, all by itself, make you one of the most efficient and effective people in your field.

Think on Paper

The power of this technique lies in its simplicity. Here's how it works: You start with a list of everything you have to do for the coming day. Think on paper.

You then place an A, B, C, D, or E next to each item on your list before you begin the first task.

An *"A"* item is defined as something that is very important, something that you must do. These items are the frogs of your life.

If you have more than one A task, you prioritize these tasks by writing "A-1", "A-2", "A-3", and so on in front of each item. Your A-1 task is your biggest, ugliest frog of all.

"Shoulds" Versus "Musts"

A *"B"* item is defined as a task that you *should do*. But it has only mild consequences. These are the tadpoles of your work life. Returning an unimportant telephone message or reviewing your e-mail would be a B task.

You should never be distracted by a tadpole when a big frog is sitting there waiting to be eaten.

The rule is that you should never do a B task when an A task is left undone. You should never be distracted by a tadpole when a big frog is sitting there waiting to be eaten.

A *"C"* task is defined as something that would be *nice* to do but for which there are no consequences at all, whether you do it or not. C tasks include phoning a friend, having coffee or lunch with a coworker, and completing some personal business during work hours. These sorts of activities have no effect at all on your work life.

A *"D"* task is defined as something you can *delegate* to someone else. The rule is that you should delegate everything that someone else can do so that you can free up more time for the A tasks that only you can do.

An *"E"* task is defined as something that you can *eliminate* altogether, and it won't make any real difference. This may be a task that was important at one time but is no longer relevant to you or anyone else.

After you have applied the ABCDE Method to your list, you will be completely organized and ready to get more important things done faster.

Take Action Immediately

The key to making this ABCDE Method work is for you to now discipline yourself to start immediately on your A-1 task and then stay at it until it is complete. Use your willpower to get going and stay going on this one job, the most important single task you could possibly be doing. Eat the whole frog and don't stop until it's finished completely.

Your ability to think through and analyze your work list and determine your A-1 task is the springboard to higher levels of accomplishment and greater self-esteem, self-respect, and personal pride. When you develop the habit of concentrating on your A-1, most important activity – on eating your frog – you will start getting more done than any two or three people around you.

When every physical and mental resource is focused, one's power to solve a problem multiplies tremendously.

Norman Vincent Peale

Chapter 7

Focus on Key Result Areas

"Why am I on the payroll?" This is one of the most important questions you can ever ask and answer, over and over again, throughout your career.

As it happens, most people are not sure exactly why they are on the payroll. But if you are not crystal clear about why you are on the payroll and what results you have been hired to accomplish, it is very hard for you to perform at your best, get paid more, and get promoted faster.

In simple terms, you have been hired to get specific results. A wage or a salary is a payment for a specific quality and quantity of work that can be combined with the work of others to create a product or service that customers are willing to pay for.

Your job can be broken down into about five to seven key result areas, seldom more. These represent the results that you

*"Why am I on the payroll?"
This is one of the most
important questions you
can ever ask and answer,
over and over again,
throughout your career.*

absolutely, positively have to get to fulfill your responsibilities and make your maximum contribution to your organization.

A key result area is defined as something for which you are completely responsible. If you don't do it, it doesn't get done. A key result area is an activity that is under your control. It produces an output that becomes an input or a contributing factor to the work of others.

Key result areas are similar to the vital functions of the body, such as those indicated by blood pressure, heart rate, respiratory rate, and brain-wave activity. An absence of any one of these vital functions leads to the death of the organism. By the same token, your failure to perform in a critical result area of your work can lead to the end of your job as well.

Clarity is Essential

The starting point of high performance is for you to identify the key result areas of your work. Discuss them with your boss. Make a list of your most important output responsibilities, and make sure that the people above you, on the same level as you, and below you are in agreement with it.

For example, for a salesperson, getting qualified appointments is a key result area. This activity is the key to the entire sales process. Closing a sale is a key result area. When the sale is made, it triggers the activities of many other people to produce and deliver the product or service.

For a company owner or key executive, negotiating a bank loan may be a key result area. Hiring the right people and delegating effectively are both key result areas. For a receptionist or secretary, typing letters and answering the phone and transferring callers quickly and efficiently are defined as key result areas. People's ability to perform these tasks quickly and efficiently largely determines their pay and promotability.

The Great Question

Here is one of the greatest questions you will ever ask and answer:

"What one skill, if I developed and did it in an excellent fashion, would have the greatest positive impact on my career?"

You should use this question to guide your career for the rest of your life. Look into yourself for the answer. You probably know what it is.

Ask your boss this question. Ask your coworkers. Ask your friends and your family. Whatever the answer is, find out and then go to work to bring up your performance in this area.

The good news is that all business skills are *learnable*. If anyone else is excellent in that particular key result area, this is proof that you can become excellent as well, if you decide to.

One of the fastest and best ways to stop procrastinating and get more things done faster is for you to become absolutely excellent in your key result areas. This can be as important as anything else you do in your life or your career.

Do what you can, with what you have, where you are.
Theodore Roosevelt

Chapter 8

Apply the Law of Three

Three core tasks that you perform contain most of the value that you contribute to your business or organization. Your ability to accurately identify these three key tasks and then to focus on them most of the time is essential for you to perform at your best. Let me tell you a true story.

Three months after her first full-day coaching session with me in San Diego, Cynthia stood up and told the group a story. She said, "When I came here ninety days ago, you claimed that you would show me how to double my income and double my time off within twelve months. This sounded completely unrealistic, but I was willing to give it a try."

"On the first day, you asked me to write down a list of everything that I did over the course of a week or a month. I came up with seventeen tasks that I was responsible for. My problem was that I was completely overwhelmed with work.

I was working ten to twelve hours per day, six days per week, and not spending enough time with my husband and my two young children. But I didn't see any way out."

"I had been working for eight years for a fast-growing entrepreneurial company in the high-tech area, but there always seemed to be an overwhelming amount of work to do and never enough time."

One Thing All Day Long

She continued with her story. "Once I had made up this list, you then told me to ask this question: 'If you could do only one thing on this list all day long, which one task would contribute the greatest value to your company?' Once I had identified that task, which was quite easy, I put a circle around that number."

"You then asked, 'If you could do only one more thing on your list of key tasks, which would be the *second* activity that contributes the most value to your company?'"

"Once I had identified the second most important task, you asked me the same question with regard to the *third* most important task."

"You then said something that shocked me at the time. You said that fully 90 percent of the value that you contribute to your company is contained in those three tasks, whatever they are. Everything else you do is either a support task or a complimentary task that could probably be delegated, downsized, outsourced, or eliminated."

Take Immediate Action

Cynthia continued with her story. "As I looked at the three tasks, I realized that these were the three things that I did that contributed the most value to my company. This was on a Friday. On Monday morning at 10 o'clock, I met with my boss and explained to him what I had discovered. I told him that I needed his help in delegating and outsourcing all my work except for those three key tasks. I felt that if I could work on those three tasks exclusively, all day long, I could more than double my contribution to the company. Then I said to him that if I doubled my contribution, I would like to be paid twice as much."

> "*Which one task would contribute the greatest value to your company?*"

She said, "My boss was completely silent. He looked at my list of key tasks, looked back up at me, looked at the list again, and then said, 'Okay'. It was now 10:21 am according to the clock on the wall behind him."

"He said, 'You're right. These are the three most important things that you do in this company – and the three things that you do the best. I will help you to delegate and downsize all these other minor tasks to free you up to work full-time on these three key tasks. And if you double your contribution, I will pay you twice as much.'"

Transform Your Life

Cynthia concluded her story by saying, "He did; then I did; then he did. He helped me delegate and assign my minor tasks so I could concentrate on my top three jobs. As a result, I doubled my output over the next thirty days, and he doubled my income."

"I had been working very hard for more than eight years, and I doubled my income in just one month by focusing all my time and energy on my three key tasks. Not only that, but instead of working ten and twelve hour days, I work from 8:00 to 5:00 and spend time in the evenings and on the weekends with my husband and my children. Focusing on my key tasks has transformed my life."

Perhaps the most important word in the world of work is *contribution*. Your rewards, both financial and emotional, will always be in direct proportion to your results, to the value of your contribution. If you want to increase your rewards, you must focus on increasing the value of what you do. You must dedicate yourself to contributing more results to your company. And three key tasks always contribute the most.

Work All the Time You Work

To keep your life in balance, you should resolve to work all the time you work. When you go to work, put your head down and work the whole time. Start a little earlier, stay a little later, and work a little harder. Don't waste time. Every minute that you spend in idle chitchat with coworkers is time taken away from the work that you must accomplish if you want to keep your job.

Even worse, time that you waste at work often has to be taken away from the members of your family. You have to either stay late or take work home and work in the evenings. By not working effectively and efficiently during your workday, you create unnecessary stress and deprive the members of your family of the very best person you can possibly be.

There is a story of a little girl who goes to her mother and asks, "Mommy, why does Daddy bring a briefcase full of work home each night and never spend any time with the family?" The mother replies sympathetically, "Well, honey, you have to understand – Daddy can't get his work done at the office so he has to bring it home and get caught up here." The little girl then asks, "If that's the case, why don't they put him in a slower class?"

No matter what the level of your ability, you have more potential than you can ever develop in a lifetime.

James T. McCay

Chapter 9

Prepare Thoroughly Before You Begin

One of the best ways for you to overcome procrastination and get more things done faster is to have everything you need at hand before you begin. When you are fully prepared, you are like a cocked gun or an archer with an arrow pulled back taut in the bow. You will be amazed at what you achieve in the months and years ahead. You just need one small mental push to get started on your highest value tasks.

This is like getting everything ready to prepare a complete meal, such as a big frog. You set all the ingredients out on the counter in front of you and then begin putting the meal together, one step at a time.

Begin by clearing off your desk or workspace so that you have only one task in front of you. If necessary, put everything on the floor or on a table behind you. Gather all the information, reports, details, papers, and work materials that you will require to complete the job. Have them at hand so you can reach them without getting up or moving much.

Be sure that you have all the writing materials, computer disks, access codes, e-mail addresses, and everything else you need to start working and continue working until the job is done.

Set up your work area so that it is comfortable, attractive, and conducive to working for long periods. Especially, make sure that you have a comfortable chair that supports your back and allows your feet to rest flat on the floor.

> "Set up your work area so that it is comfortable, attractive, and conducive to working for long periods."

Create a Comfortable Workspace

The most productive people take the time to create a work area where they enjoy spending time. The cleaner and neater your work area before you begin, the easier it will be for you to get started and keep going.

One of the great techniques for overcoming procrastination (eating frogs) is for you to get everything that you need to work completely ready, in advance. When everything is laid out neatly and in sequence, you will feel much more like getting on with the job.

Launch Toward Your Dreams

Once you have completed your preparations, it is essential that you launch immediately toward your goals. Get started. Do the first thing, whatever it is.

My personal rule is "Get it 80 percent right and then correct it later." Run it up the flagpole and see if anyone salutes. Don't expect perfection the first time or even the first few times. Be prepared to fail over and over before you get it right.

> **The biggest enemies we have to overcome on the road to success are not a lack of ability and a lack of opportunity but fears of failure and rejection and the doubts that they trigger.**

The only way to overcome your fears is to "do the thing you fear", as Emerson wrote, "and the death of fear is certain."

Wayne Gretzky, the great hockey player, once said, "You miss 100 percent of the shots you don't take." Once you have completed your preparations, have the courage to take the first action, and everything else will follow from that. The way you develop the courage you need is to act as if you already had the courage and behave accordingly.

Persons with comparatively moderate powers will accomplish much, if they apply themselves wholly and indefatigably to one thing at a time.

Samuel Smiles

Take It One Oil Barrel at a Time

There is an old saying that "by the yard, it's hard; but inch by inch, anything's a cinch!"

One of the best ways to overcome procrastination is for you to get your mind off the huge task in front of you and focus on a single action that you can take. One of the best ways to eat a large frog is for you to take it one bite at a time.

Lao-tzu wrote, "A journey of a thousand leagues begins with a single step." This is a great strategy for overcoming procrastination and getting more things done faster.

Crossing a Great Desert

Many years ago, driving an old Land Rover, I crossed the heart of the Sahara Desert, the Tanezrouft, deep in modern-day Algeria. By that time, the desert had been abandoned by the French for years, and the original refueling stations were empty and shuttered.

The desert was 500 miles across in a single stretch, without water, food, a blade of grass, or even a fly. It was totally flat, like a broad, yellow sand parking lot that stretched to the horizon in all directions.

More than 1,300 people had perished in the crossing of that stretch of the Sahara in previous years. Often, drifting sands had obliterated the track across the desert, and the travelers had gotten lost in the night, never to be found again alive.

> "One of the best ways to eat a large frog is for you to take it one bite at a time."

To counter this lack of features in the terrain, the French had marked the track with black, fifty-five gallon oil drums every five kilometers, which was exactly the distance to the horizon, formed by the curvature of the earth.

Because of this, in the daytime, we could see two oil barrels – the one we had just passed and the one five kilometers ahead of it. And that was all we needed to stay on course.

All we had to do was to steer for the next oil barrel. As a result, we were able to cross the biggest desert in the world by simply taking it "one oil barrel at a time."

Take It One Step at a Time

In the same way, you can accomplish the biggest task in your life by disciplining yourself to take it just one step at a time. Your job is to go as far as you can see. You will then see far enough to go further.

To accomplish a great task, you must step out in faith and have complete confidence that your next step will soon become clear to you. Remember this wonderful advice: "Leap – and the net will appear!"

A great life or a great career is built by performing one task at a time, quickly and well, and then going on to the next task. Financial independence is achieved by saving a little money every single month, year after year. Health and fitness are accomplished by just eating a little less and exercising a little more, day after day and month after month.

You can overcome procrastination and accomplish extraordinary things by taking just the first step, getting started toward your goal, and then taking it one step, one oil barrel, at a time.

The only certain means of success is to render more and better service than is expected of you, no matter what your task may be.

Og Mandino

Chapter 11

Upgrade Your Key Skills

Upgrading your skills is one of the most important personal productivity principles of all. Learn what you need to learn so that you can do your work in an excellent fashion. The better you become at eating a particular type of frog, the more likely you are to just plunge in and get it done.

A major reason for procrastination is a feeling of inadequacy, a lack of confidence, or an inability in a key area of a task. Feeling weak or deficient in a single area is enough to discourage you from starting the job at all.

Continually upgrade your skills in your key result areas. Remember, however good you are today, your knowledge and skills are becoming obsolete at a rapid rate. As Pat Riley, the basketball coach, said, "Anytime you stop striving to get better, you're bound to get worse."

Never Stop Learning

One of the most helpful of all time management techniques is for you to get better at your key tasks. Personal and professional improvement is one of the best time savers there is. The better you are at a key task, the more motivated you are to launch into it. The better you are, the more energy and enthusiasm you have. When you know that you can do a job well, you find it easier to overcome procrastination and get the job done faster and better than under any other circumstances.

> "Learn what you need to learn so that you can do your work in an excellent fashion."

Refuse to allow a weakness or a lack of ability in any area to hold you back. Everything is learnable. And what others have learned, you can learn as well.

When I began to write my first book, I was discouraged because I could use only the hunt-and-peck method of typing. I soon realized that I had to learn to touch-type if I was ever going to write and rewrite a 300-page book. So I bought a touch-typing program for my computer and practiced for twenty to thirty minutes every day for three months. By the end of that time, I was typing forty to fifty words per minute. With this additional skill, I have been able to write more than forty books that have now been published all over the world.

The best news is that you can learn whatever skills you need to be more productive and more effective. You can become a touch typist if necessary. You can become proficient with a computer. You can become a terrific negotiator or a super salesperson. You can learn to speak in public. You can learn to write effectively and well. These are all skills you can acquire as soon as you decide and make them a priority.

The more you learn, the more you can learn. Just as you can build your physical muscles through physical exercise, you can build your mental muscles with mental exercises. And there is no limit to how far or how fast you can advance except for the limits you place on your own imagination.

Do your work; not just your work and no more, but a little more for the lavishing's sake – that little more which is worth all the rest.

Dean Briggs

Chapter 12

Leverage Your Special Talents

You are remarkable! You have special talents and abilities that make you different from every other person who has ever lived. There are frogs you can eat, or learn to eat, that can make you one of the most important people in your business or organization.

There are certain things that you can do, or learn to do, that can make you extraordinarily valuable to yourself and to others. Your job is to identify your special areas of uniqueness and then to commit yourself to becoming very, very good in those areas.

Increase Your Earning Ability

Your most valuable asset in terms of cash flow is your earning ability. Your ability to work enables you to bring tens of thousands of dollars into your life every year by simply applying your knowledge and skills to your world. This is your ability to eat specific frogs faster and better than others.

*There are certain things
that you can do, or learn to do,
that can make you
extraordinarily valuable
to yourself and to others.*

Take stock of your unique talents and abilities on a regular basis. What is it that you do especially well? What are you good at? What do you do easily and well that is difficult for other people? Looking back at your career, what has been most responsible for your success in life and work to date? What have been the most significant frogs you have eaten in the past?

Do What You Love To Do

One of your great responsibilities in life is for you to decide for yourself what you really love to do and then to throw your whole heart into doing that special thing very, very well.

Look at your various tasks and responsibilities. What is it that you do that gets you the most compliments and praise from other people? What do you do that positively affects the work and performance of other people more than anything else?

You should always focus your best energies and abilities on starting and completing those key tasks that your unique talents and abilities enable you to do well and that make a significant contribution. You cannot do everything, but you can do those few things in which you excel, the few things that can really make a difference.

Concentrate all your thoughts on the task at hand.
The sun's rays do not burn until brought to a focus.

Alexander Graham Bell

Chapter 13

Identify Your Key Constraints

Between where you are today and any goal or objective that you want to accomplish, there is one major constraint that must be overcome before you can achieve that major goal. Your job is to identify it clearly.

What is holding you back? What sets the speed at which you achieve your goals? What determines how fast you move from where you are to where you want to go? What stops you or holds you back from eating the frogs that can really make a difference? Why aren't you at your goal already?

These are some of the most important questions you will ever ask and answer on your way to achieving high levels of personal productivity and effectiveness. Whatever you have to do, there is always a *limiting factor* that determines how quickly and well you get it done. Your job is to study the task and identify the limiting factor or constraint within it. You must then focus all of your energies on alleviating that single choke point.

Look Into Yourself

Successful people always begin the analysis of constraints by asking the question,

"What is it *in me* that is holding me back?"

They accept complete responsibility for their lives and look to themselves for both the cause and cure of their problems.

In your own life, you must have the honesty to look deeply into yourself for the limiting factor or limiting skill that sets the speed at which you achieve your own personal goals. Keep asking, "What sets the speed at which I get the results I want?"

Strive for Accuracy

The definition of the constraint determines the strategy that you use to alleviate it. The failure to identify the correct constraint, or the identification of the wrong constraint, can lead you off in the wrong direction. You can end up solving the wrong problem.

A major corporation, a client of mine, was experiencing declining sales. The corporation's leaders concluded that the major constraint was the quality of the sales force and the sales management. They spent an enormous amount of money reorganizing the management and retraining the salespeople.

They later found that the primary reason that sales were down was a mistake made by an accountant who had accidentally priced their products too high relative to their competition in the marketplace. Once the corporation revamped its pricing, its sales went back up and it returned to profitability.

Behind every constraint or choke point, once it is located and alleviated successfully, you will find another constraint or limiting factor. Whether you're trying to get to work on time in the morning or build a successful career, there are always limiting factors and bottlenecks that set the speed of your progress. Your job is to find them and to focus your energies on alleviating them as quickly as possible.

Starting off your day with the removal of a key bottleneck or constraint fills you full of energy and personal power. It propels you into following through and completing the job. And there is always something. Often, alleviating a key constraint or limiting factor is the most important frog you could eat at that moment.

The first requisite for success is the ability to apply your physical and mental energies to one problem incessantly without growing weary.

Thomas Edison

Chapter 14

Put the Pressure on Yourself

The world is full of people who are waiting for someone to come along and motivate them to be the kind of people they wish they could be. The problem is that no one is coming to the rescue.

These people are waiting for a bus on a street where no buses pass. If they don't take charge of their lives and put the pressure on themselves, they can end up waiting forever. And that is what most people do.

Only about 2 percent of people can work entirely without supervision. We call these people "leaders". This is the kind of person you are meant to be and that you can be, if you decide to be.

To reach your full potential, you must form the habit of putting the pressure on yourself and not waiting for someone else to

Only about 2 percent of people can work entirely without supervision. We call these people "leaders". This is the kind of person you are meant to be and that you can be, if you decide to be.

come along and do it for you. You must choose your own frogs and then make yourself eat them in their order of importance.

Lead the Field

See yourself as a role model for others. Raise the bar on yourself. The standards you set for your own work and behavior should be higher than anyone else could set for you.

Make it a game with yourself to start a little earlier, work a little harder, and stay a little later. Always look for ways to go the extra mile, to do more than you are paid for.

Your self-esteem, the core of your personality, has been defined by psychologist Nathaniel Branden as "the reputation you have with yourself." You build up or pull down your reputation with yourself with everything you do or fail to do. The good news is that you feel better about yourself whenever you push yourself to do your best. You increase your self-esteem whenever you go beyond the point where the average person would normally quit.

Successful people continually put the pressure on themselves to perform at high levels. Unsuccessful people have to be instructed and supervised and pressured by others.

By putting the pressure on yourself, you will accomplish more and better tasks faster than ever before. You will become a high-performance, high-achieving personality. You will feel terrific about yourself, and bit by bit, you will build up the habit of rapid task completion that will then go on to serve you all the days of your life.

Gather in your resources, rally all your faculties, marshal all your energies, focus all your capacities upon mastery of at least one field of endeavor.

John Haggai

Chapter 15

Maximize Your Personal Powers

The raw material of personal performance and productivity is contained in your physical, mental, and emotional energies. Your body is like a machine that uses food, water, and rest to generate energy that you then use to accomplish important tasks in your life and work. When you are fully rested, for example, you can get two times, three times, and five times as much done as when you are tired or burned out.

One of the most important requirements for being happy and productive is for you to guard and nurture your energy levels at all times.

Overworking Can Mean Under-producing

The fact is that your productivity begins to decline after eight or nine hours of work. For this reason, working long hours into the night, although it is sometimes necessary, means that you are usually producing less and less in more and more time.

The more tired you become, the worse the quality of your work will be and the more mistakes you will make, at a certain point, you can reach "the wall" and simply be unable to continue, like a battery that is run down.

Work at Your Own Pace

There are specific times during the day when you are at your best. You need to identify these times and discipline yourself to use them on your most important and challenging tasks.

Most people are at their best in the morning, after a good night's sleep. Some people are better in the afternoon. A few people are most creative and productive in the evening or late at night.

A major reason for procrastination is fatigue or attempting to start on a task when you are tired. You have no energy or enthusiasm. Like a cold engine in the morning, you can't seem to get yourself started.

Whenever you feel overtired and overwhelmed with too much to do and too little time, stop yourself and just say "All I can do is all I can do."

Sometimes the very best use of your time is to go home early and go to bed and sleep for ten hours straight. This can completely recharge you and enable you to get two or three times as much work done the following day, and of a far higher quality, than if you had continued working long into the night.

Get Enough Sleep

According to many researchers, the average American is not getting enough sleep relative to the amount of work he or she is doing. Millions of Americans are working in a mental fog as the result of working too much and sleeping too little.

One of the smartest things you can do is to turn off the television and get to bed by 10:00 p.m. each night during the week. Sometimes one extra hour of sleep per night can change your entire life.

Guard Your Physical Health

In addition to getting lots of rest, to keep your energy levels at their highest, be careful about what you eat. Start the day with a high-protein, low-fat, and low-carbohydrate breakfast. Eat salads with fish or chicken at lunch. Avoid sugar, salt, white-flour products, and desserts. Avoid soft drinks, candy bars, and pastries. Feed yourself as you would feed a world-class athlete before a competition because in many respects, that's what you are before starting work each day.

> *"Turn off the television and get to bed by 10:00 p.m. each night during the week."*

Aim to exercise about 200 minutes each week, the agreed-upon standard for excellent levels of fitness. This is equal to about thirty minutes per day and can be achieved by going for a walk before or after work or by walking short stretches during the day. You can swim, use exercise equipment, or play sports, but build exercise into your daily routine, just as if it were a business appointment.

The better you feel when you start work, the less you will procrastinate and the more eager you will be to get the job done and get on with other tasks. High energy levels are indispensable to higher levels of productivity, more happiness, and greater success in everything you do.

It is the compelling zest of high adventure and of victory, and of creative action that man finds his supreme joys.

Antoine De Saint-Exupery

Chapter 16

Motivate Yourself Into Action

To perform at your best, you must become your own personal cheerleader. You must develop a routine of coaching yourself and encouraging yourself to play at the top of your game.

Most of your emotions, positive or negative, are determined by how you talk to yourself on a minute-to-minute basis. It is not what happens to you but the way that you interpret the things that are happening to you that determines how you feel. Your version of events largely determines whether these events motivate or demotivate you, whether they energize or de-energize you.

To keep yourself motivated, you must resolve to become a complete optimist. You must decide to respond positively to the words, actions, and reactions of the people and situations around you. You must refuse to let the unavoidable difficulties and setbacks of daily life affect your mood or emotions.

Develop a Positive Mental Attitude

In Martin Seligman's twenty two year study at the University of Pennsylvania, summarized in his book *Learned Optimism*, he determined that optimism is the most important quality you can develop for personal and professional success and happiness. Optimistic people seem to be more effective in almost every area of life.

It turns out that optimists have four special behaviors, all learned through practice and repetition. ***First***, optimists ***look for the good in every situation***. No matter what goes wrong, they always look for something good or beneficial.

> **"**You must develop a routine of coaching yourself and encouraging yourself to play at the top of your game.**"**

2 **Second**, optimists always *seek the valuable lesson in every setback or difficulty*. They believe that "difficulties come not to obstruct but to instruct."

3 **Third**, optimists always *look for the solution to every problem*. Instead of blaming or complaining when things go wrong, they become action oriented. They ask questions like "What's the solution? What can we do now? What's the next step?"

4 **Fourth**, optimists *think and talk continually about their goals*. They think about what they want and how to get it. They are always looking forward rather than backward.

When you continually visualize your goals and ideals and talk to yourself in a positive way, you feel more focused and energized. You feel more confident and creative. You experience a greater sense of control and personal power.

And the more positive and motivated you feel, the more eager you are to get started and the more determined you are to keep going.

There is more to life than just increasing its speed.

Gandhi

Chapter 17

Get Out of the Technological Time Sinks

Technology can be your best friend or your worst enemy. As we race into the twenty-first century, bombarded by information from all sides, many people seem to have an irresistible, if not obsessive, need to communicate continually with people everywhere – in their personal and business lives.

This compulsion to communicate incessantly – entailing the nonstop use of cell phones, BlackBerry devices, personal digital assistants, the Internet (both wireless and wired), and various contact management systems such as Microsoft Outlook and Maximizer – tends to leave people psychologically breathless. We have no time to stop, smell the roses, and collect our thoughts.

The beginning of a habit is like an invisible thread, but every time we repeat the act we strengthen the strand, add to it another filament, until it becomes a great cable and binds us irrevocably, thought and act.

Orison Swett Marden

with it. Problems get solved, answers get found, work gets done, and life continues to flow along like Old Man River. Very few things are so important that they cannot wait.

Chapter 18

Slice and Dice the Task

Most of the really important work you do requires large chunks of unbroken time to complete. Your ability to carve out and use these blocks of high-value, highly productive time is central to your ability to make a significant contribution to your work and to your life.

Successful salespeople set aside a specific time period each day to phone prospects. Rather than procrastinating or delaying on a task that they don't particularly like, they resolve that they will phone for one solid hour – between 10:00 and 11:00 am, for example – and they discipline themselves to follow through on their resolution.

Many business executives set aside a specific time each day to call customers directly to get feedback, to return phone calls, or to answer correspondence. Some people allocate specific thirty to sixty minute time periods each day for exercise. Many people read great books fifteen minutes each night before retiring. In this way, over time, they eventually read dozens of the best books ever written.

And herein lies the secret of true power. Learn, by constant practice, how to husband your resources, and concentrate then, at any given moment, upon a given point.

James Allen

Chapter 21

Single Handle Every Task

Self-Discipline is the Key

Elbert Hubbard defined self-discipline as "the ability to make yourself do what you should do, when you should do it, whether you feel like it or not."

In the final analysis, success in any area requires tons of discipline. Self-discipline, self-mastery, and self-control are the basic building blocks of character and high performance.

Starting a high-priority task and persisting with that task until it is 100 percent complete is the true test of your character, your willpower, and your resolve. Persistence is actually self-discipline in action. The good news is that the more you discipline yourself to persist on a major task, the more you like and respect yourself, and the higher is your self-esteem. And the more you like and respect yourself, the easier it is for you to discipline yourself to persist even more.

You eventually feel capable of setting and achieving any goal. You become the master of your own destiny. You place yourself on an ascending spiral of personal effectiveness on which your future is absolutely guaranteed.

And the key to all of this is for you to determine the most valuable and important thing you could possibly do at every single moment and then *Eat That Frog!*

ABOUT THE AUTHOR

Brian Tracy is a professional speaker, trainer, and consultant and is the chairman of Brian Tracy International, a training and consulting company based in Solana Beach, California. He has been a highly successful entrepreneur and in 1981, began teaching his success principles in talks and seminars around the country. Today, his books, audio programs, and video seminars have been translated into thirty-five languages and are used in fifty-two countries.

Tracy has shared his ideas with more than 4 million people in forty-five countries since he began speaking professionally. He has served as a consultant and trainer for more than 1,000 corporations. He has lived and practiced every principle in this book, and has taken himself and countless thousands of other people from frustration and underachievement to prosperity and success.